Henry Seymour Conway

The Speech of General Conway

Henry Seymour Conway

The Speech of General Conway

ISBN/EAN: 9783337341909

Printed in Europe, USA, Canada, Australia, Japan

Cover: Foto ©Thomas Meinert / pixelio.de

More available books at **www.hansebooks.com**

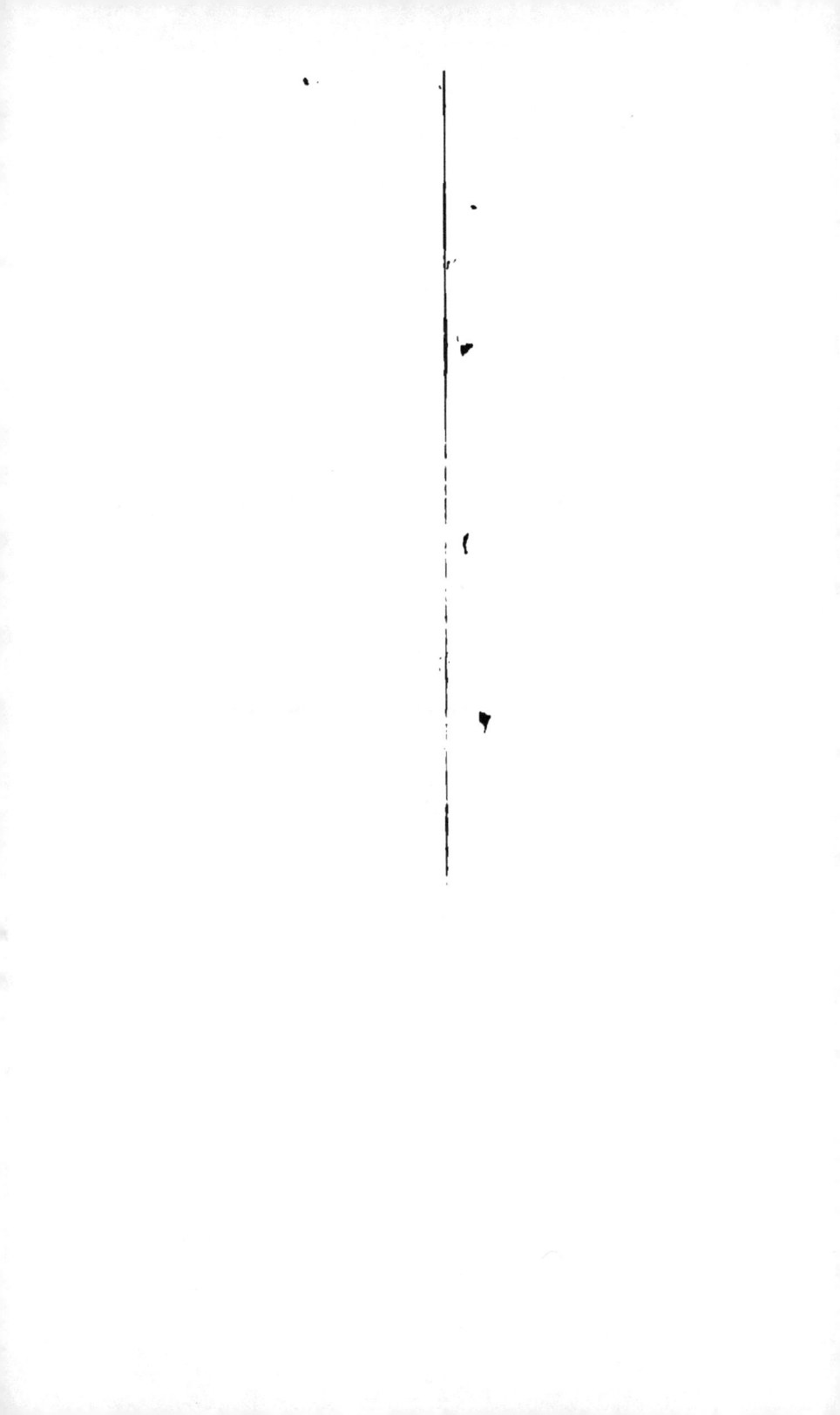

THE

SPEECH

OF

GENERAL CONWAY,

&c. &c. &c.

PRICE ONE SHILLING and SIX-PENCE.

THE

SPEECH

OF

GENERAL CONWAY,

MEMBER OF PARLIAMENT

FOR

SAINT EDMONDSBURY,

ON MOVING IN THE

HOUSE OF COMMONS,

(ON THE 5th OF MAY, 1780)

" That Leave be given to bring in a BILL for QUIETING the
" TROUBLES NOW REIGNING in the BRITISH COLO-
" NIES in AMERICA, and for enabling His MAJESTY to
" appoint COMMISSIONERS, with full Powers to treat, and
" conclude upon Terms of CONCILIATION with the said
" COLONIES."

LONDON:

PRINTED FOR T. CADELL IN THE STRAND.

M,DCC,LXXXI.

SPEECH, &c.

Mr. SPEAKER,

I SOME time ago engaged myself to this House, to bring before them a matter of great importance. But reflecting fully on the difficulties attending it, I almost repent of my rashness, for they are not only the difficulties of the subject, or its importance, great enough to deterr a man of much superior talents, but they are the difficulties of the times, the state of men, and of things; of parties, and of opinions. I stand besides in the unfortunate predicament of having a system, which, differing from the leading ideas on both sides of the House, and having no protection but from my feeble powers, is in danger of being crushed and annihilated between the collision of

B   contending

contending parties, or perhaps held in equal
contempt by both.

However, Sir, I hope this once the
House will grant me their indulgence, and
will pardon my presumption, if animated
with an ardent and sincere zeal, and the ful-
lest internal conviction, I almost flatter myself I shall relate such facts, and draw such
conclusions from them, as may make some
impression on their minds.

Gentlemen know that it is on the subject
of the American war I mean to trouble
them, and to offer to their judgment a plan
of conciliation.

But before I enter into this, I beg leave
to make some few observations on the general situation of this country, which I
will not say is the most desperate, (I hate
the word) but undoubtedly the most dangerous it was ever in, since the existence of
the British monarchy. Depressed with
debt; exhausted by taxes; our resources,
and almost our spirit, failing; with little
but our pride and passions left to support

us; involved in a dangerous and unequal war with the united force of France and Spain, while a fatal rebellion is preying upon our vitals : Such is our general calamitous fituation. But this is not all : we have not only many powerful enemies, but we have not one friend. 'Tis not France and Spain alone; all Europe feems armed, or arming againſt us. The great powers deride and defpife; even the little ones peck at and infult us. The Dantzickers; the towns of Lubeck and Hamburgh; even Holland, the *laſt lingering friend*, feems to have *bid farewel*. We are like the ſtricken deer, driven out of the herd, and may foon not have a name, or a being, among the powers of Europe. To fuch a pitch have our faults and our follies, our ignorance and our prefumption, brought us. We have deferved, and we have, I doubt, incurred the wrath of Heaven : and though we go on with annual mockeries of prayer and faſting, we fhew in our conduct no fign nor fymptom of amendment; floth and indolence, and indifference, have taken the place of manly exertion and vigilance. But

fuch

[4]

fuch are not the means of obtaining divine affiftance.

Ubi focordiæ tete atque ignaviæ tradideris, nequicquam deos implores; irati infeftique funt.

But, Sir, it is in this miferable chaos, in this ftate of darknefs, almoft under the fhadow of death, that it becomes every man, who has a heart feeling for the difgraces and diftreffes of his country, to fee if from no quarter a ray of hope breaks through the gloom. And, if my zeal does not too far betray me, I think there is one which, if now feized and purfued, may lead us out of this labyrinth; may yet reftore us to glory and happinefs.

The firft ftep to reformation is, repentance; and I would to God I faw in the minds of our governors, thofe figns of repentance, that converfion which I flatter myfelf I fee in the people. They are at laft, I think, ftarted up from that golden dream of conqueft, which fallacy and falfehood had painted to their imagination.

The

The scales are fallen from their eyes, they see how they have been sacrificed and deceived; and their songs of triumph are now turned into clamours and bitter lamentations. But, sir, they are not yet the loud cries of rage and resentment; they are the cool complaints of disappointment and apprehension; of fears and just alarms for themselves and their posterity; they behold the fabrick of their great empire, as it were, crumbling, and dissolving all around them; but instead of vengeance against the authors of their calamities, they mildly call for reformation.---'Tis not the fury of a storm, but the calm murmur of a refluent tide,

And surely, if ever the voice of the people claimed attention, it is in a moment like the present; it ought to be heard, it must be heard; and, I may say, it will be heard; it has, hitherto, spoken almost in whispers; soon, if not regarded, it may speak in thunder.

This

This nation, fir, is fick with many evils, fome of them I have touched upon; and, I am forry to fay, it is alfo blotted with many vices, and foul corruptions; but I do not mean to enter into them, they are beyond my ftrength, and they are not the bufinefs of this day; and, indeed, *" fufficient to the day is the evil thereof."* For this day is fet apart to the confideration of the American war; an evil in itfelf fo monftrous, that we muft foon conquer it, or perifh under it;

Hæret lateri læthalis arundo.

It is the fatal fhaft fticking in our fide; piercing to our vitals, and draining almoft the laft drop of our blood.

In deliberating, therefore, upon the means of reftoring peace with America; it feems to me almoft a deliberation about our own being. *" Our life and death are both before us;"* and I can fcarce help adding the other folemn words of Cato.

" This, in a moment, brings me to
" my end;
" But this affures me I fhall never die."

The

The continuation of this diftracted war is certain death to us; whereas, a happy and cordial reconciliation with America, upon fair and folid grounds,- may fix the greatnefs of the Britifh empire till time fhall be no more.

But, fir, it is a great work; it demands all your judgment to digeft, and your ut-moft vigour and exertion to atchieve. Something muft be undone, as well as done; you muft renounce many favourite maxims conceived in the hour of happinefs, and in the pride and infolence of your power; and trace back again thofe erroneous fteps that have brought you to the brink of this pre-cipice.

I do not mean to go back with much re-trofpect on the paft, nor to dwell much on any invidious or difputable matter; and fhall only touch flightly on thofe leading prin-ciples on which this war was begun, and has been purfued, as far as is necefary to lay the fubject clearly before you. The avowed principle of this war, fir, was the

taxation

taxation of America; a fyftem foolifhly, I
think, and fatally conceived, equally im-
politic and unjuft. I fhall never forget
that fatal night when this Houfe, in a thin
Committee, and in a dark and evil hour,
like a band of black confpirators, refolved
to rob three millions of Britifh fubjects of
their liberty and property; for a Refolu-
tion was .nen propofed and formed *to tax
America*. I was one of the few who op-
pofed that propofition; and then, at that
early period, warned my countrymen of
the many dangers that attended it; it is fifteen years fince; but I now feel inexpref-
fible fatisfaction in that remembrance; and
fhall carry it, with pride and confolation,
to my grave.

I will not fatigue and wound your minds
by a recapitulation of all the wretched
fcenes that have fucceeded; the faults and
follies we have committed; the contradictions, tergiverfat.)ns, deceptions, and all
the train of difgraces that have followed.
The miferable fyftem of Taxation was maintained as long as it could be maintained;
nay,

nay, I may fay, even longer; it fhewed
itfelf through fifty difguifes: firft, in the
fhape of Regulation, then the honour of
Parliament, then under the fallacious garb
of a conciliatory propofition: though it had
been, in the moft folemn and exprefs
words, renounced by Lord Hillfborough's
letter, yet ftill it was maintained; and,
when the fubftance was given up, profeffedly, we contefted for the fhadow. All
idea of any other tax but the Tea-duty was
difclaimed; but ftill the Tea-duty was
maintained; we quarrelled for the Tea-
duty, fought for the Tea-duty, for the
Tea-duty was this deftructive war with
France, Spain and America, pofitively made.
Could folecifm, infatuation, and infanity,
go farther? the Poet's accufation of our
weak firft Parent, who

" *For an apple damn'd mankind,*"

is fcarce an exaggerated expreffion for fuch
folly.

It was faid, however, if th's was a folly, t was not the folly of the minifters only, t was the folly of the nation; which I cnow was, in part, true; but I know too, vhy it was true : becaufe the people were 1ever rightly informed; becaufe a fcene of conftant deception was practifed to inflame nd mifguide them; becaufe, " a flood of ' Treafure, from American Taxation, was ' to pay their debts, and eafe all their ' burthens; becaufe the Americans were ' natural enemies to this country; Aliens, ' or Rebels and Independants, by prin- ' ciple; they were Cowards, befides; and ' a few thoufand men could, at any time, ' fubdue, and drive them off the Conti- ' nent."---Upon fuch reprefentations did he people form their opinions; upon the ıme, were built all thofe lofty and mag- ificent principles upon which this war has cen purfued; one would have the *Ame- icans at our feet*, another would *reduce them s unconditional fubmiffion*, a third *would con- uer them by ftarvation*, a fourth, *by fire and epopulation :* Thefe things were not in the ıouths of the ignorant alone; men of the

firſt

first weight, the first dignity, adopted them.
All the Law and Learning of the Kingdom were employed to inforce them.

*" The Rubicon is paſt, kill them, or they
kill you."*

Such was the ſentence of the greateſt Judge
of the land, and the firſt Oracle of Government.

With ſuch Authorities to lead, and ſuch
Viſions to inflame them, 'tis no wonder
the people took fire.----This furious ſpirit
thus kindled by the heads of the Party, *In
Patriam, populumque fluxit.* The Rage did,
I confeſs, ſeize almoſt all ranks and orders
of men; but for being more general, it
was not more juſt. It became, indeed, the
ſin of the people; but was, as I have
ſhewn, the ſin of Government firſt.

" Peccavit, et peccare fecit Iſrael."

Even the more ſacred function, and the
higheſt orders of it, caught the Frenzy
too,

too, and joined with the deluded people in
this *dance of death*.

Neither charity nor juftice, nor decorum,
in my opinion, were heard; all was paffion.

Three millions of our fellow fubjects
were condemned unheard. Sir, it was a
cafe of blood! By the ordinary rules of the
Conftitution, thofe pious fages ought not
to have had a part in it. I tread upon tender
ground: I know the refpect due to thofe
right reverend perfons, and for their piety
and learning, in their true facred character,
nobody has more: but a little too much
zeal for the meafures of the day; too much
complaifance for the authors of thofe meafures, too often miflead them. In their
diocefes I revere them; I would treat them
every where with refpect; but politicks are
not their trade, and don't do them honour:
they are a fhining body of the nation undoubtedly, and have done the higheft honour to it on many occafions; but in the

4   prefent

present times, I doubt, are a faulty, if not a rotten part of the Conftitution.

I beg pardon for this little digreffion, Sir: I faid the Americans were condemned unheard. They were truly fo, and in that I think were concentred and united all the fum and effence of our cruelty, tyranny, and injuftice: fuch a conduct furpaffes even the rancour of favages, and is unknown in the annals of civilized nations. In vain did they fupplicate, proteft, befeech, beg to be heard. You anfwered, " *They were* " *rebels*, and deferved no attention; that " they had formed a determined fyftem of " independence, and renounced the autho- " rity of the Britifh legiflature." They denied the charge, and appealed, in the moft folemn manner, to God and their country, for the truth of their affertions. 'Twas in vain ; you determined they were Rebels. You chofe they fhould be Rebels, that you might fubdue and trample upon upon them as fuch.

I do

I do not talk from hearfay, or imagination, but from the moft publick and au-
thentick teftimonials : their numerous me-
morials and petitions to parliament, and the
throne ; and their letters to the people of
Great Britain and Ireland. Thefe Sir, were
the genuine language of America; formal-
ly, properly, and conftitutionally before
you. In denying the charge of rebellion,
they difproved it : the renouncing the authority of Parliament, and applying to its
power, was a contradiction in terms.

But fuch was the dominion of paffion at
that time, that contradictions paffed for de-
monftrations, and the humbleft fupplica-
tions for declarations of war and defi-
ance.

But, Sir, to fhew I do neither miftake
nor mean to mifguide, I beg leave to lay
their declarations before you in their own
words; for it is effential to know what was,
and I believe, as far as human feelings al-
low,

low, is ſtill the diſpoſition of the Americans.

In the petition of the Congreſs to the
King, in 1775, they ſay, by removing the
grievance above-mentioned,* " *the harm-*
" *ny between* Great Britain *and their Co-*
" *lonies,* ſo neceſſary to the happineſs of
" both, and *ſo ardently deſired by the latter,*
" will be immediately reſtored.---In the
" magnanimity and juſtice of your Majeſ-
" ty and *Parliament* we confide for a redreſs
" of *our other grievances,* &c.

" For appealing to that Being who
" ſearches thoroughly the hearts of his crea-
" tures, we ſolemnly profeſs that our
" Councils have been influenced by no other
" motive than a dread of impending de-
" ſtruction. Permit us, therefore, moſt
" Gracious Sovereign, in the name of all
" your faithful people of America, with
" the utmoſt humility to implore you, for
" the honour of Almighty God, whoſe

* Taxation.

" *pure*

" *pure religion our enemies are undermining,*
" for your glory, which can only be ad-
" vanced by rendering your people happy,
" &c. &c.

" That your royal authority and inter-
" position may be used for our relief, and
" that a gracious answer may be given to
" this petition."

This petition was allowed to be moderate
and reasonable, and was laid before Parliament by Lord Dartmouth, with many other
papers that year.

The New-York Memorial to the House
of Lords, of the 25th of March, 1775,
says, " We shall always chearfully submit
" to the constitutional exercise of the su-
" preme regulating power lodged in King,
" Lords, and Commons of Great Britain ;
" and to all acts calculated for the general
" weal of the empire, and the due regula-
" tion of the trade and commerce thereof.

" We

" We conceive this power includes a
" right to lay duties upon all articles im-
" ported directly into the Colonies, from
" any foreign country, &c. &c. But that
" it is the undoubted right of our Consti-
" tution, that no taxes be imposed on them,
" but with their consent, given personally,
" or by their lawful representatives.

" We therefore hope your Lordships
" *will aid and concur in redressing* our griev-
" ances, removing all causes of dissention
" with Great Britain, and establishing our
" rights and privileges upon a solid and
" lasting foundation."

The representation and remonstrance of
the same Colony to the House of Commons.
After stating their grievances, they say,

" Nor in claiming these essential rights
" do we *harbour the most distant idea of in-*
" *dependence,* on the parent kingdom. We
" *acknowledge the Parliament of Great Bri-*
" *tain necessarily entitled to a supreme direc-*

D   " *tion*

" *tion and Government over the whole Em-*
" *pire.*

" We claim *but a restoration of that which*
" *we enjoyed before the close of the last war.*
" *We desire no more than a continuation of*
" *that ancient Government, to which we are*
" *entitled by the principles of the British Con-*
" *stitution.*

" Attached by every tye of interest and
" regard to the British nation, &c. &c. we
" harbour not an idea of diminishing the
" power and grandeur of the mother coun-
" try, or lessening the lustre and dignity of
" Parliament. Our object is the happiness
" which can only arise from the union of
" both countries.

" Fully trusting that this Honourable
" House will listen *with attention to our*
" *complaints,* and redress our grievances,
" &c."

In the Address to the People of England,
the 8th of July, 1775, they say,

" They

" They are accufed of aiming at Inde-
" pendency, which they deny, as a charge,
" *fupported only by the allegations of our Mi-*
" *niftry.*

" Abufed, infulted, and contemned,
" what fteps have we purfued to obtain re-
" drefs? We have carried our *dutiful Pe-*
" *titions to the Throne.* We have applied
" to your juftice for relief."

" It has been faid, we refufe to fubmit to
" the reftrictions on our commerce. From
" whence is this inference drawn? Not from
" our words, we having repeatedly declared
" the contrary."

They declare " their readinefs to fubmit
" to the acts of Trade and Navigation, paft
" before the year 1763.

" They are ready to fubmit to any far-
" ther acts for the regulation of their ex-
" ternal commerce----excluding every idea
" of taxation, internal or external, for

D 2   " *raifing*

" *raiſing a revenue on the ſubjects of Ame-*
" *rica without their conſent.*"

They ſay, " they had again preſented an
" humble Petition to his Majeſty; and to
" remove every imputation of obſtinacy,
" have requeſted his Majeſty *to direct ſome*
" *mode, by which* the united applications of
" his faithful Coloniſts may be improved
" into an *happy and permanent reconcili-*
" *ation.*"

That was the Petition brought over by
Mr. *Penn*, dated the 4th of *September*, 1775.

In that they farther ſay, among many
other expreſſions of loyalty and duty,

" Our breaſts retain too tender a regard
" for the kingdom, from which we derive
" our origin, to requeſt ſuch a conciliation
" as might be in any manner *inconſiſtent*
" *with her dignity, or her welfare.*"

When

When I reflect upon thefe things, and upon our conduct in confequence, they feem more like a vifion of the night, than a reality, and the public tranfactions of a great, and formerly wife nation, in the face of day. I know how many falfe and idle pretences were made; and how we fhamefully cavilled at expreffions, when matters were in queftion upon which the very fate of this country depended.---They denied our right to tax them, and they denied nothing elfe; and they expected the regul-tion of their internal concerns by their own affemblies, agreeably to the fpirit of their Charters, and to the common rights of a Free People. But becaufe they denied any thing, becaufe they refufed to be flaves, you called them Rebels; a vain Idol of dignity, the creature of our pride and avarice, was fet up: To this, our real dignity was facrificed (for Dignity cannot confift with Tyranny and Injuftice) to this, whole Hecatombs of Britifh fubjects were devoted, and the beft blood of this country daily poured out. Fitter facrifices to the beaftly

Moloch

Moloch than to the Genius of this free nation.

This is not a Government for flaves in any part of its Dominions. Philip II. faid *" he had rather have no fubjects, than be a " King of Hereticks;"* a Britifh monarch fhould fay, " he had rather not be a King, " than be a King of flaves."

I beg pardon fir; I fear I tire your patience, I have dwelt longer on this retrofpect of our conduct and fituation than I intended; I hope the zeal which has infenfibly carried me away, on a fubject I have fo much at heart, will be excufable.

I now proceed to explain to the Houfe, the plan which I propofe to offer, and the foundation upon which I have formed fome hopes of its fuccefs, fhould it meet with your approbation.

Firft, fir, it is a Parliamentary plan. I propofe to fpeak to the Americans by the voice of Parliament; and to lay down

grounds

grounds and terms of Conciliation pre-
vioufly fanctified and ratified by Parliament.

Several plans of reconciliation have, at
different times, been propofed in Parliament; but all, fucceffively, rejected; I
fhould indeed except one, that of the noble
Lord below me, very improperly called *a
Plan of Conciliation*; for it was, in my
humble opinion, the very Antipodes of
Conciliation. It was a plan of virtual and
effectual Taxation, and confequently to-
tally inadmiffible by the Americans; it
was a plan for the noble Lord's favourite
dignity; and confequently not a plan to
gain the hearts of our Colonifts;

" *Non bene. conveniunt et in unâ fede mo-*
          " *rantur,*
" *Majeftas et Amor.*"

Such dignity did not confift with the love
of that free people; you could not both
take their money, and win their hearts;
but it was imagined they might be capti-

vated with words, and think the found of freedom, as good as freedom; indeed, to thofe to whom Liberty is but a name, it may be fo; *they* judged by more ftubborn principles, they held their own property faft; but *that* fincerely and folidly fecured, during all the firft periods of the conteft, their hearts were yours. This I fhall for ever maintain as a demonftration. The fcene is undoubtedly changed, and we have now the difficult tafk before us of retrieving an almoft loft game; by fo much the more difficult, as to regain the love of a much injured friend, is harder than to win the affections of a ftranger.

But, I faid this was a Parliamentary plan; it was by Parliament I propofed this great work of peace fhould be done; by Parliament alone I think it can be done; and furely, fir, it is among the capital folecifms of the times, that while the Honour of Parliament was oftenfibly, indeed oftentatioufly, held out as the caufe of quarrel, all final fettlement was conftantly taken out of the hands of Parliament, and made

made the bufinefs of the Crown and its
Minifters;---but, fir, for a Parliamentary
fettlement, every reafon feems to me to mi-
litate. The voice of Parliament, fpeaking
by an Act of Parliament, is the voice of
the nation; that voice is fteady, folid, permanent, not fhifting and fhuffling, like the
voice of Minifters. The voice of Parliament will be trufted by the Americans;
the words of Minifters, it is plain, cannot; it is, befides, more for our dignity,
that Parliament fhould declare, and fix the
general grounds upon which fhe means to
accept of the friendfhip of the Colonies, or
grant them hers; than that we fhould wait
to hear them from thence. But above all
the reft, is the great expediency, almoft
neceffity, of a *fudden conclufion:* our fituation will not bear procraftination, the delay of a fingle year, nay a fingle month,
may be fatal to us, not from the miferable
wafte and decay of our ftrength alone, but,
as in the prefent critical difpofition of
things new events may happen, or new
enemies arife to make that fituation ftill
more defperate. This plan, fir, is framed

E   for

for the speediest conclusion; for it holds
out terms which the Americans at large, or
any particular province, may accept when
they will, and be immediately *at his Majesty's peace*; not a day, scarce an hour,
need be lost in that desirable work; no
previous negociation is needful; to signify
their consent is sufficient.

As to the particular terms, I have followed, pretty nearly, Lord Chatham's plan,
but with some variations in the matter and
manner; and it is a subject of pride to me,
that I tread, though at an humble distance,
in the steps of that great man, and true
friend to his country.

I mean by it to remove all their just
complaints, and to grant them all their
just demands; to make their own petitions, in general, the ground of our con-
cessions; to secure them all their rights,
their liberty and their property, not grudg-
ingly, but fully and freely; not slightly,
nor precariously, but irrevocably; not de-
pendent upon the caprice of any Minister,
but

but bound by the faith of the British Parliament.

It is a standard to which they may at any time repair; an asylum and bulwark to which they may resort; and a boon and grace given in perpetuity, and which it is not even left to their own failings or weakness to forfeit.

Such is the principle and scope of the Bill I shall presume to offer to the House; and to save their time in hearing a more detailed description of the particular terms, I will, with their permission, though not agreeable, I believe, to strict Parliamentary form, read, or beg the Clerk may be allowed to read, the Bill, as I have drawn it up. It may have, it has, I make no doubt, many defects; but I am not tenacious of particular words, or terms; take from it, add to it, mold it according to your wisdom,---it is yours from this moment, tho' I confess my darling child: I offer it to your care, but let me recommend it to your indulgence.

" To

" *To you, Sirs, and your honours, I be-*
" *queath it.*"

Form it, fashion it, as you please; but do
not cut the babe in twain; leave it that vital
principle; that spirit which alone can make
it an honour to its parent, or an advantage
to the publick.

There remains now but one consideration
more, though that a most important one;
namely, what hopes we have any reasonable
ground to form of its success: And here,
Sir, I know the many difficulties the subject labours under, and how many adverse
opinions I have to struggle with: some are
for no terms, no offers at all: some will
think them too large: some are for withdrawing the troops, and some for giving
absolute independence. I know besides the
difficulty of obtaining any peace in our present situation; but I beg the House to re-
collect that if the difficulty is great, the
prize is inestimable.

As to withdrawing the troops, or grant-
ing independence, I shall say little. The
former

former has the air of a poor and cowardly yielding, leaving them all their force un-controlled, and their league with France and Spain entire. ΄ The latter I think a dreadful alternative, for should the Thir-teen Colonies be severed from us, we may still, perhaps, exist as a people, never as a great people. In the dying words of Lord Chatham, " *it is a total dismemberment of* the " Britifh Empire ; that empire which his " Majefty received entire from his progeni-" tors, and which was guaranteed to the " heirs of the Princefs Sophia." " The " Prince of Wales (he faid) might demand " his inheritance."

In fhort, Sir, it is a ftep I think little fhort of defpair fhould drive us to, and no-thing without an abfolute renunciation of their league with the Houfe of Bourbon.

As to the other, *of offering no conditions at all*, whoever thinks this is a wound *enfe recidendum*, to be cured by the fword alone, errs fatally in my opinion ; we have tried

that

that experiment too long, and there is neither common fenfe nor humanity in it.

But, Sir, I fay *the fword alone*, I never denied the ufe of the fword fince the war began ; I never refufed any aid to the full employment of it. On the contrary, I have urged, and do now, the employment of it with more activity and vigour.

There is no medium in war, and there is neither honour nor humanity in a lingering one. I would not keep one fuperfluous man at home, nor delay a moment reinforcing your armies there to the utmoft; ten thoufand men at leaft fhould immediately reinforce Sir Henry Clinton. I don't know what fo many troops are now doing at home, no way wanting to your defence. I would not lofe a moment in fending them.

What I defire is, that the alternative may be fully and fairly before them : let the picture of the famous artift be actually and conftantly prefented to their view ; on the one fide, the *horrors of war* ; on the other,

the

the certain bleffings of peace. Let the golden
Hefperian fruit be placed, not only within their fight, but within their reach. For,
Sir, they cannot tafte of it but we muft
partake. As to the probability of fuccefs,
I am not too fanguine. I faid, I faw a *ray
of hope*; I think I do: but if I could not
prove a great probability, it fhould fuffice
(to fhew the expediency of this meafure)
that *none is more probable*; that it is fafe and
honourable, the terms being of your own
dictating, and that the experiment, which
I have often urged, has never been tried.
Great terms, indeed, were offered by his
Majefty's Commiffioners, but they were not
fpecifically authenticated by Parliament. I
think the Americans wanted faith in them,
and they wanted fubfequent ratification.

Sir, I do not fay the Americans will accept thefe conditions. I am not fo pre-
fumptuous; yet I think there are many rea-
fons why they may accept them. I de-
fcribed, I think, truly, the wretched fituation of this country. But, Sir, the Americans *are not upon a bed of rofes.*

If we have difficulties, fo have they; if we have diftreffes, they are not exempt from them. I don't pretend to meafure our mutual difafters, nor to determine which muft fink and expire firft. I believe their perfonal diftreffes are much greater than ours, and their refources much lefs; but they have great and potent allies, who fupport them, and we have none.---But to what degree, and in what manner thofe allies will continue to fupport them, it feems effential to know. Will their *great and good ally*, the King of France, affift their credit, and pay their debts? I hear they already owe three hundred million of dollars; that they have very little money, and their paper currency exceffively difcredited.---By a late order of Congrefs, forty dollars currency are to be paid for one filver dollar.

The quotas now demanded from the different States are very great; their troops are ill paid, ill fed, and ill cloathed; and from hence a great difficulty in keeping them together. I have been told the men in Wafhington's army, in the Jerfeys, were laft win-
ter

ter some days reduced to live on half a pint of peas, and many had not shoes to their feet.

If these things are so, which I am not responsible for, but have some ground to believe, their *good and great ally seems* rather slow in supplying them. And this protection *of their liberties* does not, I believe, prevent much arbitary proceeding and tyranny in their rulers. Should such distresses therefore continue and increase; should their demands on France be refused, who knows but they too may *wake from their golden dream*, like ourselves, and see in this *Protector of Liberties*, the designing conqueror, and the perfidious ally?

I understand, indeed, that the French are now preparing to send them a corps of troops: But I believe that is not the mode of supply they have most wished for; stores, provisions, necessaries, and above all, money, have been the constant objects of their demands hitherto. That of sending troops has long been a measure of great

F   doubt

doubt and deliberation. I am not fure the Americans do not think, that *when they afk for bread it is giving them a* SERPENT: I know it is the opinion of fome French, and many more Americans. I do not fpeak at random; I have heard and feen opinions of great weight on that head: One I will name to you, Monfieur du Portail, a man of rank and character; and as they are very ftrong and very appofite, I will quote to you fome lines out of as fenfible a letter as I ever read; it is a letter from that gentleman to Monfieur de St. Germain, at that time Minifter of the War department in France, written above an year ago. His words are:

" It may be afked, whether it would
" not be better to fend a body of twelve or
" fifteen thoufand men hither, *Ce feroit le*
" *vrai moyen de tout gâter.* That would be
" the true way to fpoil all. Thefe people
" here, though at war with the Englifh,
" hate the French much more than the
" Englifh; and notwithftanding all that
" France has done, or might do for them,
" they would prefer a reconciliation with
" their

" their ancient brethren.----This (fays he)
" we prove every day; and fhould they for
" a moment confent to French troops com-
" ing among them, their natural antipathy
" would foon difclofe itfelf, and would
" produce the moft fatal quarrels."

And, fpeaking afterwards of the idea of
putting the French in poffeffion of Canada,
he adds:

" The neighbourhood of the French is
" fufficient to give them a diflike to their
" liberty, becaufe they would not expect
" to keep it long: Dependence for depend-
" ence, they prefer that of England."

He makes many other remarks on the
ftate and difpofition of America, very well
worth attention, and much confirming fome
propofitions I have already thrown out.
He fays,

" They want *ftores and neceffaries of many*
" *kinds, cloth, linen, leather, cordage, falt,*
" *fugar, brandy,* &c. And that thefe things

" were

" were of the more confequence, becaufe
" thefe people before the war, though not
" living in actual luxury, had all the con-
" veniences of life in great abundance;
" loved their eafe and their indolence;
" their pipe of tobacco, and their tea.
" That they were heartily grieved to be-
" come foldiers all of a fudden, and to be
" plunged into the rigours and hardfhips of
" war, which they detefted.

   " This may feem (fays he) a ftrange lan-
" guage; but fuch is really the turn of this
" people; they act with no energy, vigour,
" nor paffion in the caufe they have efpoufed,
" and continue in it only becaufe they have
" been once fet a-going in it. *Il y' a cent*
" *foit plus d' enthoufiafme pour cette re-*
" *volution cy dans un caffé de Paris, que*
" *dans toutes les Colonies Unies.*

   " There is a hundred times more enthu-
" fiafm for this revolution in a coffee-houfe
" at Paris, than in all the United Colo-
" nies."

Such

Such, Sir, are the genuine reflections of this gentleman: I do not affert the infallibility of Monfieur du Portail; I do not fwear by Monfieur du Portail; but I think he writes like a man of fenfe; he was then converfant with the Americans; he had an high rank in their army, and he feems by his ftile to have been confidentially employed to ftudy, and report to the French Minifter the ftate of things in that country.

I fhould add too, that after all thefe obfervation he urges ftrenuoufly the fupport of the American war in a proper way; and *that*, " becaufe he thinks the independence " of America would *annihilate the Marine* " *of Great Britain,* and throw its com- " merce into the hands of France."

To fome it may feem ftrange, Sir, that I, profeffedly a favourer of the Americans, and a determined enemy to this war, fhould in any degree accept fuch language, fhould exprefs fuch averfion to the Independence of America, and with a plan of conciliation in my hand, (and God knows at my heart)

heart) fhould yet urge the increafe of our army there, and the more fpirited and vigorous profecution of hoftilities.

First then, let me fay, that it is becaufe I hate the war that I am for carrying it on with vigour. If I wifhed to prolong the war, I fhould be for carrying it on ignorantly and flimfily.

And I defire it may be remembered, that although to America perfecuted our cruelty, and trampled on by our pride; to America, goaded and forced into rebellion, I was an ardent friend, yet to America irrevocably, as her Congrefs afferts, leagued with France and Spain, our natural enemies, againft us, I have long ago declared, if I am a friend to Great Britain, I muft be an enemy.

If, therefore, they are determined to be French, and not Britifh Colonies; if they will have unconditional fubmiffion from us, bad as our fituation may be, I will not think it defperate.

Defpair

Despair is a mean and cowardly vice; destruction for destruction, I would fall manfully at least, and as our great deliverer King William said, "*Die in the last ditch.*" But, Sir, you have a vast army in America; I believe the establishment is above seventy thousand men, though we have fought our principle battles with 10, or at most 15,000; whereas could we have an army of 30,000 assembled, I am persuaded the Americans never could have drawn, or kept together, one to face them; we have besides the great advantage of powerful detachments, by means of our navy, for small ones will always be both cruel and ineffectual.

Yet, Sir, I would not have you rely on the war: I would only make it subservient to the great work of peace: if I knew a possible way of making peace without it, I would abandon it.

It is, however, as I have said, but an alternative; it cannot, I think, be more fairly or honourably offered, and till it has

been

been difproved by trial, I cannot but have an hope of its fuccefs. For this plan, at the fame time that it offers them our friendfhip, proves our fincerity, and it has this peculiar advantage, that it will be always before their eyes, in all difpofitions, under all circumftances : other offers may be made on either fide at untoward times, in moments of irritation or partial advantage, and may fhift and vary with the moment. This will be out of the hands of Minifters, and out of the reach of caprice ; and however rooted the Congrefs may be in their plan of Independence and French connexion, I cannot but think there is in many of the people a diflike to that connexion, and in many more a cordial affection towards their Parent State, not yet obliterated by our ufage.

There are befides, if I am rightly informed, divifions of another kind among them, more particular and perfonal ; divifions of faction, enmity, and ambition ; no body knows how far thefe, or the influence of weighty and able men, in the army or the

4   provinces

provinces, may lead. There are, befides what I have before mentioned, the love of eafe, the wearinefs of the war, and the preffure of diftreffes.

It is from fuch caufes, and in fuch fituations, that the moft fudden and unexpected revolutions have been brought about; no lefs than five or fix in Europe, and within little more than a century paft. Two moft remarkable in our own country, the reftoration of monarchy under Charles the Second, and the happy revolution of 1688. Nor were thofe of Portugal, Denmark, and now lately of Sweden lefs fudden, or entire. In all thefe cafes the change was eafy and inftantaneous, almoft like the fcenes of a drama.

In all it was a flying from prefent evils, from the uneafinefs and preffure of the moment, and in feveral a change apparently to a ftate of lefs conftitutional liberty.

I have tired your patience; I have but one word to add, it is above all things to

G   deprecate

deprecate delay and procraftination; it is to beg that whatever you refolve, for war or conciliation, may be immediately refolved. The time is ..itical and precarious; the fcene fickle and fhifting; a moment gained may be your falvation; a moment loft, your ruin. A defeat at fea; a difafter in America; the acceffion of new enemies, (not an impoffible event) I doubt, may difable you from making war or peace. Even while we are debating, important and precious moments are ftealing away,

Dum loquimur fugerit invida
Ætas, carpe diem quam minimum credule
poftero.

I thank the Houfe for the indulgence they have fhewn me, and I humbly move, Sir,

" That leave be given to bring in a Bill
" for quieting the troubles now reigning in
" the Britifh Colonies in America, and for
" enabling his Majefty to appoint Commif-
" fioners, with full powers to treat, and
" conclude upon terms of conciliation with
" the faid Colonies."

APPENDIX.

A B I L L

FOR

Quieting the Troubles now reigning in the BRITISH COLONIES *in* AMERICA, *and for enabling his Majesty to appoint* COMMISSIONERS, *with full Powers to treat and conclude upon Terms of* CONCILIATION *with the said Colonies.*

" WHEREAS a ruinous and unna-
" tural war has for some years raged be-
" tween Great Britain and the several British
" Colonies in America, destructive at once
" of that harmony and mutual affection
" which had so long made the happiness
" and strength of both countries, and there-
" by giving every advantage to the known
" enemies of the British empire in all its
" parts, the fixed union of which had, by
" their cordial and effectual efforts, raised
" the name of Britain to the highest pitch
" of human renown and felicity ; and had,
" during the course of many glorious

G 2   " reigns

" reigns, ferved as a barrier to the liberties
" of Europe, and as the ftrongeft fupport
" of the Proteftant religion againft the
" baneful fchemes of Popery and Defpo-
" tifm.

" And whereas, in the heat of a conten-
" tion, haftily begun, many pernicious
" maxims have been adopted, and many
" falfe and dangerous meafures purfued on
" both fides.

" Now, in order to heal the faid fatal
" diffentions, and to ftop the farther effu-
" fion of fellow-fubjects' blood,

" Be it hereby declared and enacted by
" the King's moft excellent Majefty, by
" and with the advice and confent of the
" Lords, fpiritual and temporal, &c.

" That immediately upon the conclufion
" of any treaty of conciliation between
" Great Britain and America, all thofe
" rights, ~~privileges~~, and immunities, which
" were demanded by the feveral affociated
" Colonies in their Petitions and Memo-
" rials

" rials to the King, and to the two Houſes
" of Parliament, (and particularly in the
" Petition of the Congreſs to the King of
" the 8th of *July*, 1775, and in the Me-
" morial of the Colony of New-York to
" the Houſe of Lords of the 25th of
" *March*, 1775; and in the Repreſentation
" and Remonſtrance of the General Aſſem-
" bly of the ſaid Colony of New-York, to
" the Houſe of Commons of the ſame
" date,) be, and are hereby declared to be
" conceded, and confirmed on the part of
" Great Britain, to the ſeveral aſſociated
" Colonies, or to any one or more of them,
" who ſhall agree on terms of conciliation
" as aforeſaid, with any Commiſſioners ap-
" pointed, or to be appointed by his Ma-
" jeſty for that purpoſe.

" And that no doubt may remain of the
" ſincere and friendly intentions of Great
" Britain, and of her earneſt deſire to bring
" back the ancient affection of her chil-
" dren, and reſtore that beneficial inter-
" courſe which muſt ever be the true baſis
" of their grandeur and happineſs ;

4   " Be

" Be it hereby declared and enacted by
" the authority aforesaid, that from the
" day such conciliation, or treaty, shall be
" concluded, all or any of the 13 associated
" Colonies, so agreeing on terms of con-
" ciliation as aforesaid, shall be, and are
" hereby declared to be at the peace of his
" Majesty, and restored to the usual inter-
" course of friendship and commerce.
" And it is hereby farther declared and
" enacted, That no tallage, tax, or other
" charge whatever, shall from thenceforth
" be raised on the freemen of America,
" without their own consent, by their re-
" presentatives duly convened in assembly
" there.

" That the powers of the Admiralty,
" and Vice-Admiralty Courts, be restrain'd
" within their ancient limits, and the tri-
" al by jury, in all civil cases, where the
" same may have been abolished, restored.

" That no subject in America shall, in
" *capital cases*, be liable to be indicted and
" tried for the same in any place out of the
" province

" province where fuch crime fhall have
" been committed; nor be deprived of a
" trial by his Peers of the vicinage.

" That it fhall not be lawful to fend
" perfons indicted for murder in any Colo-
" ny of America, to another Colony, or to
" Great Britain, for trial.

" The Judges in the Law Courts in the
" Colonies, fhall hold their offices and fala-
" ries as *his* Majefty's Judges in England.
" *Quam diu fe bene gefferint.*

" That the Colonies in America are juft-
" ly en' 'ed to all the privileges, franchi-
" fes, ι.. _ .mmunities, granted by their fe-
" veral charters and conflitutions; and that
" the faid charters or conflitutions ought
" not to be invaded or refumed, unlefs for
" mifufe or fome legal ground of forfei-
" ture.

" And for the faid, and other good
" and beneficial purpofes, it is hereby
" declared and enacted, that the following
" acts,

" acts, or so much of the same as have
" been reprefented to be found grievous
" to the fubjects in the Colonies as afore-
" faid, namely, the acts of 4 Geo. III.
" ch. 15 and 34. 5 Geo. III. ch. 25.
" 6 Geo. III. ch. 52. 7 Geo. III. ch. 41
" and 46. 8 Geo. III. ch. 22. 12 Geo.
" III. ch. 24. 14 Geo. III. ch. 54.

" Be and are hereby repealed with re-
" fpect to all or any of the faid Colonies,
" from the day they fhall have refpectively
" entered into and concluded terms of con-
" ciliation with Great Britain, or with any
" perfons authorized by his Majefty for
" that purpofe.

" The faid acts alfo to be fufpended, and
" remain, without effect, in like manner,
" fhould any truce take place for a limited
" time between Great Britain, and all or
" any of the faid Colonies refpectively,
" during the continuance of fuch truce.

" And be it farther declared, that the
" act of 14 Geo. III. ch. 83. for regu-
" lating

" lating the government of the province
" of Quebec, fhall be reconfidered, altered,
" or repealed.

" And that no future doubt or jealoufy
" may remain relative to the rights of the
" Colonies, and the power of their affem-
" blies, lawfully conftituted, be it declared
" by the authority aforefaid, that the faid
" Colonies, in their faid affemblies, fhall,
" agreeably to their charters and conftitu-
" tions, have full power and authority to
" regulate all matters for the peace and
" good order of their internal government;
" the Legiflature of Great Britain referv-
" ing only to itfelf the power of ordering
" and enacting fuch things as concern the
" maintenance of the faid charters and con-
" ftitutions, the general weal of the em-
" pire, and the due regulation of the trade
" and commerce thereof, upon thofe prin-
" ciples of equity and found policy, which
" fhall, on full difcuffion and confideration,
" be found moft conducive to the general
" good.

II   " And

" And that nothing may obftruct or re-
" tard the great work of peace, his Ma-
" jefty is hereby authorized to appoint
" Commiffioners, with full powers to
" treat and conclude, either peace or truce,
" with all or any of the faid Colonies,
" upon fuch other, or farther terms of
" conciliation, as to his Majefty, in his
" wifdom, fhall feem fit : always under-
" ftood, and the fame is hereby again de-
" clared and enacted; that all the feveral
" privileges, immunities, and advantages
" hereby granted to all, or any of the faid
" Colonies as above-mentioned, do ferve
" as the bafis of fuch treaty of conciliation,
" and are hereby fanctified and guarantied
" under the faith of Parliament, as necef-
" fary parts of the fame.

" And farther, be it declared and en-
" acted by the authority aforefaid, that it
" fhall and may be lawful for his Majefty
" to empower Commiffioners to grant
" free pardon to any perfon, or any number
" or defcription of perfons, or his full and
" general pardon to the inhabitants of all,

4   " or

" or any of the faid Colonies refpectively,
" for all acts of hoftility, and for all things
" done or committed during the prefent
" troubles, and previous to the figning or
" conclufion of any treaty of conciliation
" as aforefaid; and the fame fhall be con-
" fidered, and is hereby confirmed as an
" act of perpetual amnefty and oblivion of
" fuch acts of hoftility, and of all things
" fo done and committed during the con-
" tinuance of the faid troubles."

THE END.

E R R A T A.

Page 1, The fentence, " I ftand befides in the unfortunate predica-,
" ment of having a fyftem," &c. fhould be read thus :—
" I ftand befides in the unfortunate predicament of having
" adopted a fyftem," &c.
—— 14, 3d line from the bottom, for principles, read privileges.
—— 47, 5th line from the end, for mifufes, read mifufer.

www.ingramcontent.com/pod-product-compliance
Lightning Source LLC
Chambersburg PA
CBHW021640270326
41931CB00008B/1094